Pollination with Mason bees
A Gardener and Naturalists' Guide to Managing Mason Bees for Fruit Production

By Margriet Dogterom

First Edition

A BEEDIVERSE BOOK

Pollination with Mason Bees

A Gardener and Naturalists' Guide to Managing Mason Bees for Fruit Production

COPYRIGHT © 2002 by Dr. Margriet Dogterom

Cover design © 2002 Wen Lin & Margriet Dogterom

Photos of bees © 2002 Sallie Sprague

Line drawings © 2002 Andrea Lonon

First edition

BEEDIVERSE ™ BOOKS
Suite 44, Unit 11 - 555 Clarke Rd,
Coquitlam, BC V3J 3XO
Canada

Beediverse.com
cpc@intergate.ca
Fax 604 936 3927
1- 800- 794-2144

National Library of Canada Cataloguing in Publication Data
Dogterom, Margriet, 1946-
  Pollination with mason bees : a gardener's guide to managing
mason bees for fruit productions
1st ed.
Includes bibliographical references and index.
ISBN 0-9689357-0-2
1. Orchard mason bee. 2. Bee culture. I. Title.
SF539.8.O73D63 2002   638'.12 C2001-904161-6

Printed in Canada
ISBN 0-9689357-0-2:   **$ 12.95 Canadian**   **$ 8.95 US   Softcover**

Table of contents

Preface

The idea to write this book came from both enthusiastic gardeners and their questions "What do I do now with my Mason bees?", and the absence of a "How to" book on managing mason bees for the backyard gardener. This is the first book on Mason bees for the lay person that includes information on nest construction and mason bee population build-up. The demand for mason bees comes from the lack of healthy honey bees with its effect of poor pollination and low fruit yields.

The title of this book uses the old term 'Mason Bee' for the early spring pollinator *Osmia lignaria* Cresson. 'Mason Bee' aptly describes their nesting activity of gathering mud to plug up their nest. Some species plug up their nests with a mastication of leaves. In North America, it is also known as 'Orchard Mason Bee' and 'Blue Orchard Bee'.

This book is organized as a hands on resource. Chapters 2 through 6 cover the major focus of this guidebook - practical information on caring for, sustaining, and increasing the mason bees in your garden. Chapter 1 provides information on pollination and its effect, how bees are important pollinators, and how to distinguish bees from wasps and flies. Chapter 7 gives the reader background on mason bees, other solitary bees, and social bees.

The purpose of this book is to guide the reader into the world of bees, and in particular, mason bees.

Acknowledgements

My sincere thanks go to all my friends, associates and workshop participants who encouraged me to write this book about how to look after mason bees. The chapters of this book grew out of the many questions I answered on the web, over the phone and at my mason bee workshops. Thus, the contributor list is long.

In particular I would like to thank the following: Victoria Bennett, Jordi Bosch, Mike Burgett, Jim Cane, Irm Dogterom, Tim Frizzell, Magna Glosli, Gorden Kern, Jenny Lakeman, Andrea Lonon, Melissa Martiny, Patricia Rathbun, Mona Reaume, Bob Smith, Rosetta Smith, Sally Sprague, Bill Stephen, Bertha Verstegen, John Vigna, David Ward and Rex Welland.

Also, a thank you to Henri Fabre who captivated my attention and curiosity with his delightful writing on solitary bees.

A Guide to Further Reading, includes the textbooks I consulted.

All have contributed, but my ideas came from the experience of keeping bees, in particular mason bees.

Chapter 1
Introduction to Bees

" ....No matter-and it shows no small courage on my part-the gyrations are duly accomplished in the presence of this unexpected witness. Then I retrace my steps and walk westward of Serignan. I take the least-frequented paths, I cut across country so as, if possible, to avoid a second meeting. It would be the last straw if I were seen opening my paper bags and letting loose my insects! When halfway, to make my experiment more decisive still, I repeat the rotation, in as complicated a fashion as before. I repeat it for the third time at the spot chosen for the release....

The distance, therefore, is, roughly, two miles....

I let them loose at quarter past two.

When the bags are opened, the Bees, for the most part, circle several times around me and then dart off impetuously in the direction of Serignan, as far as I can judge. It is not easy to watch them, because they fly off suddenly, after going two or three times round my body, a suspicious-looking object which they wish, apparently, to reconnoitre before starting. A quarter of an hour later, my eldest daughter, Antonia, who is on the lookout beside the nests, sees the first traveller arrive. On my return, in the course of the evening, two others come back. Total: three of my Masons home on the same day, out of ten scattered abroad."

In 'The Mason-Bees' by J.H.Fabre, 1916, pp 90-92

Fabre began observing mason bees in 1843, and his work was subsequently translated by A. T. DE Mattos in the beginning of the last Century. These translations have made Fabre's observations of bees and other insects more accessible to a broader audience and have delighted many naturalists and biologists. Today our curiosity is magnified by our interest in pollination.

If you are a backyard gardener in North America, you may have noticed a decline in your fruit production. Over the past 4 to 5 years, in many city and suburb gardens, inadequate pollination has been the cause

From plentiful fruit to few fruit.

for fewer and smaller fruit. This is because we have depended on the wild honey bee for pollination- and now, their colonies have been decimated by two parasitic mites (Varroa and tracheal mites).

Beekeepers do manage honey bee colonies in the city, but many municipalities prohibit beekeeping within municipality boundaries. It is clear that without wild honey bee colonies, there are insufficient bees to pollinate the many blossoms on our fruit trees.

Bees in the city.

Fortunately, native mason bees can help restore the former

productivity of your fruit trees, blueberries and raspberries. Simply, provide a nest for mason bees and they will reproduce and pollinate your fruit trees. This book will describe how to house, feed and manage mason bees.

What is pollination and why is it important?

Pollination is the key factor that determines whether the flower is fertilized and becomes fruit. More pollen delivered to a flower, means larger fruit. Simply, pollination is the transfer of pollen from one flower to another. More specifically pollen is transferred from the male part of a flower, the anther, to the receptive stigma on the female part of a flower - the pistil. With bees, pollination occurs when they visit flowers to gather pollen and nectar. Once the pollen is delivered to the flower, pollen grains send male pollen tubes down the stalk of the pistil. The genetic material from pollen is transported via the pollen tube to the female ovary where fertilization takes place.

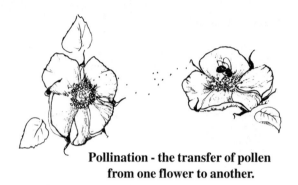

**Pollination - the transfer of pollen
from one flower to another.**

Research has shown that a minimum number of pollen grains are needed to ensure fertilization, and also the amount of pollen helps determine how big the fruit may become. After fertilization, the fertilized ovule develops into a seed. Thus, seeds in fruit are the result of fertilization through pollination. Fruit develops in response to the hormonal stimulation of fertilization. In other words, more bees = more pollen delivered = more fertilization = more and larger fruit.

1.1 WHAT IS A BEE?

Bees are insects that collect pollen on their pollen carrying hairs. Their branched and plumose hairs, present over their body parts, allows bees to collect pollen from flowers. The remaining hairs are simple (not branched).

Pollen is used to feed and nourish young developing bees. Pollen is the 'meat' that provides proteins and fats to build and maintain body structure.

Bees have a variety of specialized structures to carry pollen back to the nest. Pollen is collected amongst the hairs of a bee and is then groomed into these specialized structures (pollen basket or corbiculae in honey bees). Honey bees and bumble bees pack pollen into a pollen basket located on their hind legs, whereas mason bees pack pollen amongst hairs located underneath their abdomen (scopa). To read more about the relatives of mason bees see Chapter 7.

A mason bee visiting a flower.

A very close relationship exists between flowers and bees. Bees obtain their food from flowers, and many flowers depend on bees and other animals to pollinate their flowers. It is a fact that some flowers are so specialized they can only be pollinated by one species of bee, but generally flowers are pollinated by many bee species. This is because flowers and bees have evolved together over millions of years. The flower produces pollen and honey which attracts the bee, thus ensuring pollination, and the bee receives food as a reward, thus ensuring that it can reproduce.

In addition to pollen, flowers provide nectar, usually found inside and at the base of a flower. Nectar contains sugars which is a bees' energy source. Bees search for nectar by probing flowers. They quickly learn the easiest way to obtain nectar from the often hidden nectaries. While probing flowers for nectar, bees usually come in contact with pollen.

Bees are distinguished by their 3 body segments, 6 legs and 4 scale-free wings. Their body consists of a head, containing the eyes, mouth-parts and antennae. Wings and legs are attached to the middle part of the body or thorax. The third body segment consists of the abdomen. The female bee has an ovipositor, for laying eggs, which also functions as a stinger. The male bees have male genitalia instead of an ovipositor. In other words no male bee can sting.

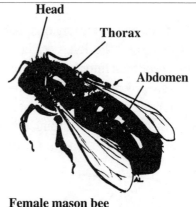

Female mason bee

1.2 IS IT A BEE, WASP OR FLY?

Bees and wasps are closely related insects that evolved from a common ancestor. The major difference between bees and wasps is that bees with their specialized branched and plumose hairs, obtain their protein from pollen, while wasps obtain their protein from meat (other insects). The specialized branched and plumose hairs are absent on wasps and they appear relatively hairless or sparsely haired.

Wasps usually obtain their protein by feeding on other insects, larvae or adults, or eat meat at your picnic. Similarly to bees, wasps forage for sugar from flowers, pop bottles, decaying fruit or any other sugary substance.

Flies often mimic bees in colour and shape, but can easily be distinguished from bees and wasps by having a close look at their antennae. Bees have a pair of antenna made of rod-like segments. A fly often has a club-shaped antennae with a tiny hair or bristle attached to the end of each club. This hair is often barely visible. The absence of a rod shaped antennae is a indication you are looking at a fly and not a bee. Blue-bottle flies look a lot like mason bees, but their habitat is usually on refuse, not on blooming flowers.

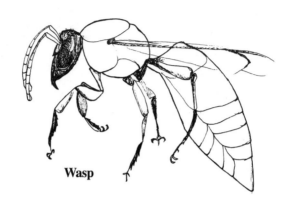

Wasp

Bees have rod-like, segmented antennae

Flies have one thin bristle attached to each antenna club

13

Chapter 2
Mason Bees

Mason bees are solitary bees grouped with the *Genus Osmia* (Panzer). Solitary means that each female nests without the cooperation of other female bees. She chooses a nest, provisions the nest and produces the young by herself. It is small to moderate, about the size of a honey bee. They are black or metallic blue-green, sometimes brilliant. While they are common in western North America, they are rare in deserts, moderately common in eastern North America, and uncommon in Mexico. There are about 135 species of mason bees.

Osmia lignaria Cresson, also known as the blue orchard bee, or orchard mason bee, is the species that is commonly present early in the spring.

Since the 1970's, research has determined that the North American mason bee can be managed for pollinating crops. Populations of mason bees

Osmia lignaria **foraging on an apple blossoms.**

can be increased and their parasites and predators controlled. These bees successfully pollinate tree fruits such as apple, cherry and almond, and berry bushes such as blueberry.

Mason bees are fun to watch

The most delightful writings by the naturalist, J. Henry Fabre (translated by A. T. DE Mattos, 1916) clearly demonstrate that bees are fun to watch. Through his writings we experience some of the delights in watching nature follow its course. One of his stories is particularly intriguing. During his teaching career, Henry Fabre took his students outdoors to teach them trigonometry. It was the students' favourite course since it meant a day roaming the countryside, albeit in straight lines. He would send his stu-

A close -up view of mason bees at their nests.

dents out to a point, pacing as they travelled, but his students kept on bending down and sticking items in their mouths. Of course this meant that the trigonometry was forgotten. Fabre investigated these antics and found to his pleasure that his students were collecting honey from the 'Mason bees of the stones'.

2.1 LIFE STAGES THROUGH THE YEAR

In winter, adult bees remain inside their cocoons. In spring, adult bees chew their way out. Bees in the outer chambers will emerge first and are usually males. They are followed by bees in the deeper chambers, usually females. Mason bees will normally emerge between late February and May. *O. lignaria* do not become active until daytime temperature reaches 14°C (57°F).

Spring

After the males emerge, they hang around the tunnel entrance, flying very little as they wait for the females to emerge. Males can be identified by the white facial hairs on the front of their face, and their long antennae - longer than the length of their head.

Mason bee emerging from her nesting tunnel.

After several days of warm weather, females begin to emerge. The female can be distinguished from the male by the absence of white hairs on the front of the face and her short antennae.

The male at this time is sexually mature and immediately mates with the newly emerged virgin female. After mating, the new mother bee searches for a suitable nesting site. Once she finds a nest cavity, she begins foraging to provision her nest. It is during this foraging process she inadvertently pollinates the flowers she visits. She collects pollen and at the nest she mixes it with nectar to form a pollen lump. When she has collected enough to feed a developing larva, she lays an egg on top of it. She then closes off the nest cell, with either mud, plant, or mixtures of plant and mud materials. She again will forage for pollen and nectar, create a new pollen lump, lay her egg and close off the nest cell. She will continue this pattern of foraging, provisioning the nest cell, laying an egg and closing off the nest, until she lays all of her eggs, or until she dies.

A male mason bee waiting for a female to emerge from the nesting tunnel.

Summer

Each egg hatches into a larva or grub. It feeds on the pollen nectar lump gathered by the female mason bee. As it eats, the larva grows. Growth of the developing larva largely depends on ambient temperature. When it is fully grown, the larva begins a resting phase (no feeding occurs at this stage). It then spins a cocoon, changes into a pupa and eventually by the end of the summer, it develops into an adult bee inside the cocoon. This transition into adulthood occurs during the summer for *Osmia lignaria*. By September the cocoons contain adult bees.

A female mason bee chooses a nesting tunnel after mating and begins foraging.

Fall and winter

Both male and females remain in their respective cocoons

18

until the warmth of next year's spring. The female cocoons are usually larger than the male cocoons. Male cocoons are located in the outer most cells or close to the entrance of the nest, and females are located in the innermost cells or away from the entrance.

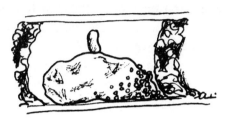

**The mason bee egg is placed on
top of the pollen-nectar
lump inside the nesting tunnel.
The female then plugs
up the tunnel with mud.**

The winter period is quite hazardous to the bees. Insect eating birds, such as woodpeckers, are known to wipe out whole populations of mason bees.

**Adult mason bee in cocoon
protected by mud partitions.**

2.2 NEST REQUIREMENTS

Mason bees need small dry nesting holes without a second entrance. They will nest in any potential nesting hole made of material such as wood, masonry, or plastic. Cavities in any material is a potential nest site although some materials are preferred over others.

Mason bees prefer 7.5 mm (5/16th") in diameter. However, they nest in both smaller and larger nest cavities.

In natural settings, mason bees will use holes created by other animals such as beetles and woodpeckers. They, also use holes such as old nail holes and counter sunk holes. Complicated structures such as key holes and electrical outlets are used if simpler nesting sites are not available. Cedar siding, whether vertical or on a slope such as a roof, is used also. Bees nest in the gap created between cedar shakes placed side-by side. The gap is usually less than 2.5 cm (1") between adjoining shakes. Another nesting spot used is the gap left between a window and the window frame; usually adjacent to weather stripping. Opening the window certainly destroys these carefully laid eggs.

In old brick and mortar buildings bees will nest in cracks formed by rotten masonry.

Mason bees may use keyholes as a nesting site if nesting holes are in short supply.

Structures such as homes and sheds provide many potential nesting sites. However, unmanaged bee populations go through major fluctuations in numbers as they go through pest and parasitic cycles. Learning how to keep parasitic populations low (see Chapter 6, Overwintering and Emergence of Cocoons) and bee populations high (see Chapter 5, Preparing Nests for Spring) will enable gardeners to have sufficient

**Mason bees nesting between
cedar shakes on a house.**

mason bees for pollinating their fruit trees every year. To learn about building your own artificial nest structure see Chapter 4 (Choosing Your Nest Type).

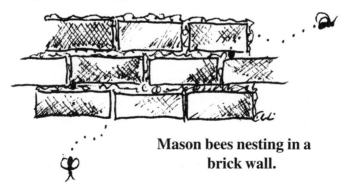

**Mason bees nesting in a
brick wall.**

2.3 FOOD FOR MASON BEES

Food in the form of nectar and pollen is the essential requirement for mason bees to feed themselves and provide food for their developing young. If food is abundant and available during the full length of the nesting period, bees will be more productive than if they have to search for their food away from their nest. In other words, bees will live longer and produce more offspring with abundant and continuous bloom in your garden. Take note of the month when there are lots of flowers and where blooms are lacking. Learn from other gardening friends and garden centres which blooms would be suitable for a particular time-frame. Search for plants on a sunny day. The presence of bees will be a good indicator of which flower are beneficial to them. If there are not enough flowers to provide food, your bees will search elsewhere for flowers. On a personal note, many of my neighbours thank me for my abundant pollinators. Note that blooming flowers sprayed with insecticides will kill bees.

Chapter 3
Getting Started with Mason Bees

Having mason bees for pollination, and being able to watch them, is possible by simply fastening a nest to an outside wall of a building. A garden is not needed in order to have mason bees. A nest can be hung on a veranda of a town-house or an apartment building. Mason bees have successfully been kept on the fourth floor. However, the 18th or the 30th floor of an apartment build-

ing may not work too well for mason bees. Placing a bee-box is just like setting out a bird box. In the spring, see if the local bees find and occupy your nest. Having mason bees come to your bee nest, is similar to having wild birds come to your bird nest. A bat house, bird house or a bee house is eventually filled with its respective occupants.

3.1 NEST AND NEST PLACEMENT

Make or buy a nest. Make sure the nesting holes are at least 13 - 15 cm (5 - 6") deep. This ensures that the correct proportion of males and females are produced. Shorter nesting tunnels produce abundant males and few females. The result is that fewer females produce fewer offspring for next year's pollination. For further information on nest types, see Chapter 4 - Choosing Your Nest Type.

Place the nest in the sun, and out of wind and rain. An east (preferred) or south facing wall of your house or shed works well. See Chapter 5 - Preparing Nests for Spring.

3.2 FINDING MASON BEES

When mason bees are not present in the home location, nests can be set out at several locations in your home region, and then brought back to the home garden. It is recommended to not go outside your home region, since pests and parasites could be brought into your home region and devastate the local mason bee population.

In British Columbia, mason bees from the Lower Mainland and Vancouver Island are available, from their respective regions, in garden store. For other regions, collect bees by setting out nesting units in early spring and wait for wild bees to lay their eggs in these nests. At the end of the summer, nesting units are brought back home. Harvesting bees from the wild is unlikely to remove all wild bees from a region since wild bees nest in natural nest sites as well as artificial nesting units.

If the number of wild bees is not known in any one area, set out 5 to 10 nests through a region. Set out one nest every half kilometre (2/3 mile), preferably adjacent to a permanent water site, such as a creek or pond. Hang nests on old buildings, protected from winds and rain, and preferably facing east. In cooler and more northerly climates, avoid hanging nests on posts (increased air currents lower temperatures) or trees (shade decreases air temperatures). In warmer climates, such as Alabama, Arizona and Utah, posts and trees are successful places for nest placement. Abundance varies between regions. In the Lower Mainland of British Columbia, mason bees are found mainly in the suburbs, probably because of both the increased availability of garden flowers for food and nesting sites in man-made structures. However, in some locations such as Utah, mason bees are equally as common in the wild.

3.3 PROVIDING FOOD

You have provided the bees with nests, now they need flowers to provide them with pollen and nectar (food). If a garden has few blooms, bees will go into the surrounding area and search for flowers. There are a few indications that mason bees will not go further than 2-3 city lots. Provide continuous bloom for your bees, which translates into lots of offspring for next year and improved pollination when they emerge from their nest the following spring.

3.4 PROVIDING A MUD SOURCE

Mason bees need mud to build walls between the eggs, and to create a plug at the terminus of the nesting tunnel. These mud walls are used to keep predators and parasites out. Usually, mason bees find a source of mud in the vicinity of the nests. Provide a mud source created by digging a hole into the mineral soil of your garden. Create several rough areas along the walls of the hole and bees will use these rough areas to begin excavating mud for their nests (see Chapter 5.2 for more details).

Chapter 4
Choosing your Nest Type

Artificial nesting units set out by home owners provide nesting habitat for wild mason bees. These nests increase the number of bees in your yard.

This chapter will help to determine the advantages and disadvantages of different nests for mason bees. As noted in Chapter 2.2, mason bees will use all types and shapes of cavities. They cannot be too fussy because they may run out of time and not be able to reproduce. Reproduction is the reason they go to work every day. A nest can have as few as one or as many as 50 + nesting holes. Nests can be a set of nesting trays or holes drilled into a log.

Wood working tools make it possible to make your own nest. Without woodworking tools, making a nest is possible by rolling paper. Whatever nest is chosen, bees will nest and pollinate flowers. The potential result is a larger fruit harvest than without bees.

Holes drilled into log

You may want to try a variety of nests. All types of housing attract mason bees, some more than others. The fun part is seeing what the bees are doing. Is there bee activity in some nests and not in others? Which nest type is more attractive to mason bees? Which nest type produces the most cocoons?

4.1 KEY MEASUREMENTS

The key measurement of mason bee nests is the inner diameter of 7.5 mm (5/16") of the tunnel. In order to increase your bee population, use a 15 - 20 cm (6 - 8") length. Shorter tubes will lead to a greater proportion of males. Usually, the front 8 - 10 cm (3 - 4") is allotted to males and the remainder is for females. In other words, if the tunnel depth is 8 -10 cm (3 - 4") your bees will be mostly male which will lower the rate of reproduction.

4.2 NEST MATERIALS

Wood and paper are the materials of choice for mason bees. Styrofoam, plastic and ceramic nests are not favoured.

Wood
Bees prefer holes that are clean and free of wooden slivers. Wooden nesting channels can be routered or cut with a table saw, or drilled into 2 adjoining pieces of wood. Holes also can be drilled into wood.

Tray Nests
Tray nests are created from pieces of wood with channels cut into one side of each tray, and stacked on top of each other. Each tray measures 15 cm (6") long, 9 cm (3 ½")wide, and 1.9cm (¾") deep. Wooden trays are placed on top of each other with the grooves facing vertically. The top tray is a blank piece of wood to

form a lid over the channels. Trays are tightly held together with bolts or tape, to prevent predators from entering nesting tunnels.

Trays - routered

Routering is done to within 1 cm (1/2") of the end of each piece of wood. Channels are created with blind holes (open only at one end). Three channels are clustered on one side, and three

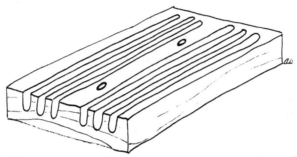

**A single nesting tray with six routered nesting channels.
The two holes are for bolting a set of trays together
into a single nesting unit.**

channels are clustered on the other to leave a space in the centre for bolts. Trays can be taped or bolted together to create a tight seal between nesting trays and prevent light from entering from the side. If some wooden trays are warped, taping with black tape will stop light from entering nesting channels. An alternative method is to have trays inside housing to prevent

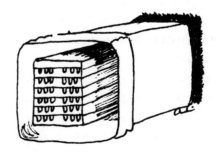

**Trays can be bolted or taped together
and housed to keep nesting
trays out of the rain.**

light from entering the trays.

Trays - Cut with Table Saw

Square channels can be cut into a piece of wood by passing it over the table saw with a Dado blade. Usually the cut is made into a full length of wood 1.8 - 2.4 m (6 - 8') as it is difficult to create a blind hole using this method. After channels have been made, the length of wood is cut into 15 cm (6") long pieces.

After aligning the trays, tape them together with masking tape. The trays will require some kind of housing or backing material so that light and predators cannot get into the back of the nesting tunnel. Tape a piece of cardboard onto the back of the stack of trays to create dark, blind tunnels. If both ends of the channels are open, bees will not nest. Fix black tape over any gaps between edges of the nesting trays.

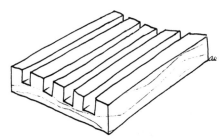

Trays cut out with a table saw

Advantage of trays

The biggest advantage of trays is that they can be dismantled and examined. Then, the number and type of bees can be identified and the nest can be cleaned to prevent the spread of disease through the use of dirty nesting tunnels. In the fall, *Osmia lignaria* cocoons can easily be removed and cleaned to avoid the buildup of parasites, and nesting trays can be washed and prepared for the following spring. The tray system allows for the removal of predators, and parasites (see Chapter 6) and increase your bee population, higher than is normally observed in nature.

Observation Trays

Plexi-glass can be mounted on single trays and used as observation hives. Trays from used nests can be used as a classroom tool to teach students about mason bees and their predators. Observation trays can be used to observe bees develop through the season and to watch bees at work. Female bees can be watched entering and exiting their nesting tunnels, and activities monitored to see what she has accomplished at day's end, or track larval development (see Hallett in Guide to Further Reading).

Drilled Holes

Mason bees nest in drilled holes of wooden blocks, but be aware of the disadvantages of this nest type. Drilled holes cannot be cleaned and as a result mite levels increase and bee production decreases - if the same blocks are used year after year without sterilisation.

A block of wood or laminate can be drilled using a 7.9 mm (5/16th") drill. However, most drills are too short to drill a hole 15 cm (6") deep. The hole can be drilled to 10 cm (4") depth and can then be drilled with a hand held drill to the 15 cm (6") mark. A brad point drill works the best if your drill operates at a slow speed, because it cleans the hole while it is being drilled. Holes cut into wood must be smooth and free of splinters.

The number of holes drilled into a block of wood can vary from few to many. The main disadvantage of numerous nesting holes is that bees have difficulties finding their nests. Difficulties in relocating their nesting holes can also happen with as few as 25 nesting holes set 1" apart. Bees could spend an inordinate amount of time searching for their nest holes. Nest markers can be added to help bees find their way back home. See Section 5.3 on providing readily recognizable nests. Extra time spent on finding home means less time gathering nectar and pollen, pollination flowers and laying eggs.

One variation of drilling holes into a large block of wood is to drill a few holes into the side of a board 2.5 x 2.5 x 15 cm (1 x 1 x 6"). A stack of these boards is inserted into a container. In the fall, each block can be given to a neighbour. Be cautious in giving or receiving, nests or straws filled with cocoons. This method of moving bees to another property may include moving parasitic mites and predators of mason bees. If you want to purchase bees, buy from a reputable supplier, someone who provides healthy, pest free stock from your home region.

Paper / Cardboard Straws

Mason bees readily use nests made out of paper or cardboard straws with an internal diameter of 7.5 mm (5/16"). Nesting straws can be made from manufactured cardboard straws or home-made newspaper straws. For both types, wrap the bundle with foam or newspaper for insulation. This prevents young developing larvae from dying under hot spring conditions.

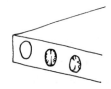

Holes drilled into small blocks of wood.

Making commercial cardboard bundles

Manufactured cardboard straws are about 33 cm (13") long. The walls are usually 0.5 mm (20/1000") thick. Look for straws with an inner diameter of 7.9 mm (5/16th"). Create a blind tunnel by crimping a 2.5 mm (1") area in the approximate centre of each straw. Use a pair of pliers to prevent straws from tearing. Bend each straw in the crimp area. Bundle 10 - 15 bent straws, making sure that all ends face in the same direction. It is beneficial if the end of the straws are uneven in length as they can find their nests more easily. Hold the bundle of straws together with an elastic band and wrap packing tape around the bundle.

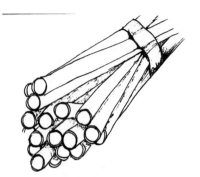

Bundle of cardboard nesting straws held together with tape.

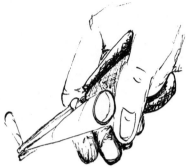

Crimp cardbooard straws to create two blind nesting tunnels.

Making hand-rolled straws bundles

This method was introduced to the author by Research Associate, Wei Shuge (Shijiazhuang Fruit Tree Research Institute, Hebei, China). Roll your own mason bee nesting straws with a 7.9 mm (5/16th") diameter, 25 cm (10") long metal or wooden dowel. Cut 18 x 5 cm (7 x 2") segments of plain white paper and longer pieces of newspaper. Using the white paper first (you don't want ink next to the nesting hole), roll both types of paper around the dowel to create a 1.8 cm (7") long tube. Secure the final roll with small amounts of tape. Liquid glue also works, but glue makes it difficult to unroll straws when harvesting cocoons in the fall. Ease the dowel out of the centre of the tightly rolled paper tube when the end of the tube has been secured.

When there are 20 straws, hold them together with an elastic band. Wrap the bundle with packing tape, leaving the holes

33

exposed. Next, cut a 15 x 15 cm (6" x 6") piece of paper. Coat one side of it with glue and wrap glue coated paper around one end of the bundle of rolled straws. Cut a piece of cardboard the same diameter as the bundle of straws. Glue the cardboard to the base of the

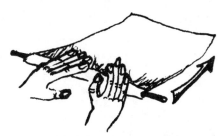

Making paper straws by rolling paper around a 5/16th inch dowl.

bundle to make the tunnels light-proof. Wrap bundle of straws into a piece of insulation. A roll of re-cycled newspaper or insulation protects bees from overheating during summer temperatures.

Paper inserts

Paper straws or inserts are available for cardboard nesting straws and drilled nesting holes in wood. These inserts are placed inside cardboard straws or wooden blocks with drilled holes. In-

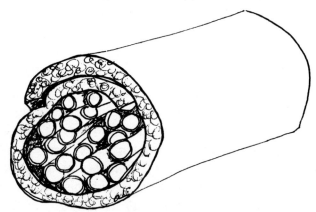

A bundle of straws bundled into a piece of insulation.

serts are removed from their housing together with bee cocoons in the fall. Inserts are disposable and are destroyed once the cocoons have been removed. In the spring, new inserts give the bees clean nests. Examine nests for mites. If mites are present, nests will require cleaning prior to inserting the new paper inserts.

Plastic

Plastic drinking straws are also potential nesting sites for mason bees. However, bees prefer cardboard or wooden nests over plastic nests. About 20% fewer cocoons were harvested from plastic straws inserted in drilled blocks of wood. Bees appear to have difficulty entering plastic nesting tunnels. If plastic straws are inserted into the wooden block so that they are recessed, bees have less difficulty entering. However, the number of cocoons harvested are equally low. Bees did not nest in bundles of white plastic straws. It is likely that bees did not use these bundles because of excessive light throughout each straw in addition to the slippery nature of plastic straws.

Styrofoam

Styrofoam nests are made for nesting alfalfa leafcutter bees that are used as commercial pollinators of alfalfa. In my own experience, the mason bee, *Osmia lignaria* does not use Styrofoam nesting tunnels whether created from trays or solid Styrofoam.

Natural

There are many plants with hollow stems that are used by nesting bees. Reeds in marshes make useful nests. Some mason bee enthusiasts have harvested reeds and set them up in shelters at home for their mason bees. The following plants have also been observed to house mason bees: *Juncus, Sorbus spp.*, cane and bamboo. Inert material such as concrete, rocks, and snail shells are also used as nest structures to house mason bees.

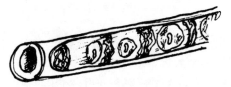

**A natural reed tube used
by mason bees as a nesting
tunnel. Small pollen lumps
with eggs are partitioned off
from each other.**

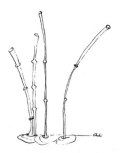

**Reeds can be harvested
for use as mason bee
nesting tunnels.**

Chapter 5
Preparing Nests for Spring

The most important part of spring management is to have a nest ready for bees. They will be looking for nesting sites in early spring, several weeks prior to spring bloom. For coastal British Columbia, Canada, set nests out in February and earlier in southern regions. On the west coast of British Columbia, natural emergence occurs when the flowering shrub *Pieris japonica* begins to bloom, usually after willow and before dandelion. See Chapter 4 on Choosing Your Nest Type, and choose the nest best suited to the needs of your garden.

5.1 NEST PLACEMENT

Place nests in the vicinity of your garden. The best location for bees to produce many offspring is not always obvious. If nest location, weather, and food is optimal, the rate of increase can be six times the original mason bee population. It is through foraging that the bees pollinate the flowers. Time available for foraging can be increased by making mud available to the nest and by placing nests close to bloom. Similarly, the use of contaminated nests from the previous spring is counterproductive due to parasitic mite build-up among the offspring. Check Chapter 6 for methods of cleaning and harvesting cocoon.

Pollination with Mason Bees

Location

The best nest location is above ground, in the sun, protected from wind and rain, and facing east. When nests face east, the early morning sun will warm up the nest and bees. The bees will start foraging earlier than if the nest faces west, or, even worse, north. Bees will use nests facing directions other than east. However, mason bees that live in a north-facing nest won't begin foraging until mid-morning, when ambient temperatures warm to 16°C (61°F). Therefore they will have less foraging time. Avoid placing nests on fence posts or on a fence because air movement around the fence lowers the air temperature and may decrease the number of hours your bees are at work. Bees need the sun to warm up before they can start pollinating your fruit trees. Placing a nest in the shade, on the north side of a building, or in the shade of a tree all decrease a bees' foraging activity. On the other hand, placing nests in the sun may be detrimental in the hotter, drier and in the more southern states of the U.S. Therefore, noon or afternoon shade in hot climates may be desirable.

Height

Attach the nest 1.5 m (5') high on a wall of a shed or your house. This is a good height for observing your bees flying to and from the nest. Bees will use nests placed at or near the ground or higher than 1.8 m (6'), but it is more difficult to observe them.

Distance

Place the nest as close to flowering trees as possible. Within 70 m (225') works well. Bees need a supply of food and pollen material reasonably close to the nest. The greater distances that bees have to travel, between their nest and foraging patch, the less pollinating is completed. The best combination is where the food source and the trees that need pollination are close to the nest.

Moving nests

Once the nest is placed out in early spring, do not move it until the end of the nesting season or early summer. Leaving the nests throughout the summer increases parasitism and predation. Do not move them during foraging season, as outbound females will become lost and not find their way home. Moving nests early in spring and summer may dislodge the developing larvae from its pollen provisions. The larvae will then starve and die. In addition, jarring the nest, or dropping the nest in the summer may damage the developing bee inside the cocoon. If a nest has to be moved, take the nest unit from the wall, and put it with the entrance facing skyward, so any dislodged larvae are likely to fall back on their food mass. Move it to the new storage location without jarring it. In September, the nest can be held in a non-heated storage garage or garden shed until the nest and cocoons are cleaned or moved to next year's spring location.

5.2 MAKING MUD AVAILABLE TO BEES

Mason bees need mud to plug up their nests and to construct partitions between each egg laid on its pollen provisions. Mud is

**Watching mason bees collect
mud from a hole dug into
to the mineral layer of the soil.**

used to seal their newly laid eggs from predators and parasites. Their time gathering mud is time away from foraging (i.e. pollinating) so you want them to have a mud source nearby.

Provide bees with a mud source by digging a hole 30 x 60 x 30 cm (1 x 2 x 1') within 15 m (50') of the nest and into mineral soil. If soil is dry, add water to hole to moisten soil. As a result, bees spend more time on foraging and pollinating your fruit blossoms. You may observe bees collecting their muddy load, and then flying back to the nest. Note that bees excavate caverns into side walls of the mud hole to obtain their mud.

If your garden soil consists of gravel and sand, an artificial mud hole can be created. Dig a hole 60 x 60 x 30 cm (2 x 2 x 1') and collect several buckets of mud. Place plastic ice cream bucket at the bottom of the hole. Fill the bucket to overflowing with clay. Pour water into the bucket on a weekly basis. Water from the bottom of the bucket will permeate up through the clay to moisten it. Bees only collect mud with the 'correct' moisture content.

5.3   PROVIDE READILY RECOGNIZABLE NESTS

When a bee begins foraging for pollen and nectar, she requires various cues to orient herself back to the nest entrance. Decorating the front of a nest makes it easier for bees to find their own nesting tunnel. A nest can be decorated with simple designs and or with one or two colours. Too few or too many markers at the nest entrance will confuse bees. Bees that are confused by the markers or lack of markers close to their nest can be observed flying in and out of several nesting tunnels or getting thrown out of neighbour's nesting tunnels. They spend valuable pollinating time flying around seeking their nesting tunnel. Yellow, mauve, pink and blue are good colours for marking the front of each nest. Simple designs painted across the face of a nest helps a bee find her way back to her nesting tunnel. Some simple designs are shown here.

L   I   V   X   O

Paper and cardboard straws can be decorated by painting the end of a few straws with light coloured paint. The unevenness of straws in a bundle is an additional cue for bees returning to the nest.

5.4 PROTECT NEST FROM PREDATORS

Nests and their contents can be protected from woodpeckers by crimping chicken wire over the front of each nest. woodpeckers have a long tongue, so place firm chicken wire with 2.5 cm (1") diameter holes around the front of the nest, 5 - 8 cm (2 - 3") away from nesting tunnels.

Other predators of bees are ants, squirrels, bear and humans. Ants are particularly a problem in southern Interior of United States and more recently in California. Both the fire ant and the Argentinian ant will devastate colonies of bees, including ground nesters, above ground nesters and honey bee colonies. One solution to problematic ants is a trap with Tanglefoot®, a commercially available sticky substance that does not dry out when set outside. Dr. Jim Cane from University of Utah, has created a unique method of keeping ants off bee nests. A tennis ball is cut in half and punctured in the center of both halves. The lower half of the tennis ball is filled with Tanglefoot® and the upper part of the tennis ball acts to protect the container of Tanglefoot® from filling up with rain water. Both halves of the tennis ball are skewered onto the conduit pipe. Jim Cane, also suggests that an area can be tested for potential ant problems by setting out a few baits. Baits are made from honey smeared onto some paper. In regions with a high ant populations ants find honey within minutes.

5.5 PROTECT NEST FROM RAIN

Nests and their contents can be destroyed by rain. Protect the nesting unit with a good roofing material like cedar. The whole nest can also be placed in either a ceramic or plastic container that is big enough to shelter the whole nest. Attaching a square plastic bucket on its side works well. If the container is white or light in colour, paint it black or dark brown. Bees tend to prefer nests that are placed in sunny locations with shaded interiors. The shaded nesting tunnel can be created with a overhanging roof. It is advisable to drill holes at the bottom of plastic buckets or other containers to allow for some ventilation and avoid excessive humidity.

5.6   NUMBER OF NESTING TRAYS

The number of empty nesting tunnels needed in your garden depends on the number of mason bees present. More mason bees are usually found in gardens with old buildings, sheds, dead snags and/or around houses with cedar shingles, siding and roofs. If mason bees have been observed in the garden, set out several nests. Place nests in different locations to increase the chance of wild mason bees finding the nest. Initially, in most gardens, one nesting structure with 25 nesting holes will be sufficient.

If the number of cocoons harvested in the fall is known, the number of nests required in the following spring can be calculated with some certainty. For example, 100 cocoons harvested in the fall, have about 45 females (normally about six males are produced for every five female). On average, each female mason bee uses about one nesting tunnel . With six nesting tunnels per wooden tray eight trays (48 nesting tunnels) are needed for 100 cocoons. This calculation may seem simplistic, but on average, in a good year, one female only requires one hole. If a female lays all it eggs (about 30), she would need about five nesting tunnels. However, birds, spiders, and cars all take their toll. The majority of female bees only live for about three weeks. Some live shorter and some longer. A few may live for eight weeks. The offspring of these 100 cocoons could number from 250 to 1000, but because of various hazards your carefully tended mason bee nests will likely only yield about 300.

Chapter 6
Overwintering and Emergence of cocoons

Fall management includes cleaning cocoons and nests in preparation for setting out in early spring. The purpose of cleaning cocoons and nests is to maintain bee numbers sufficient to pollinate the fruit trees in the garden. If bees and their nests are not cleaned on a yearly basis, bee numbers increase and decrease over the years, as in all natural cycles. The result is that pollination and fruit harvest will also be variable. The number of bees can be increased or at least maintained by keeping predators and parasites numbers low. Cleaning both nest and cocoons is one way to decrease the number of parasites. It is recommended to clean both cocoons and trays every year.

6.1 HARVESTING COCOONS

Cocoons are easily harvested from nesting trays, but it is more time consuming and awkward

Trays are easily disassembled by unbolting and separating trays.

removing them from nesting straws. When removing cocoons from trays or cardboard straws, cover your work site with a large piece of newspaper to contain debris and fragmented mud removed from each nest.

Nesting trays

Open nesting trays by removing bolts or tape. Trays can then be examined one at a time.

Remove cocoons from each tray by using a small plastic coffee stir stick. Simply wedge stir stick underneath cocoon and lever cocoon out of tray. If tray is held vertically, and supported on a counter, a stir stick can be pushed vertically down under cocoons lined up in each nesting channel. If a section of the nesting

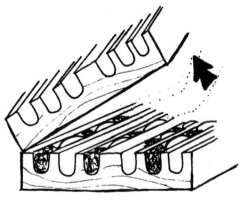

Mason bee cocoons are easily harvested from nesting channels by separating one tray from another.

tunnel is filled with mites (reddish sand-like material) remove cocoons while leaving majority of mites behind in nesting tunnel. Separating mites from cocoons at this stage will significantly reduce washing time. After cocoons have been harvested, set trays aside for cleaning.

Paper or Cardboard straws

It is more time consuming to harvest cocoons from cardboard or paper nests than from nesting trays. Cocoons are removed from straws by making a small cut in one end of the straw with a sharp utility knife. Then cardboard or paper is unravelled from this point and cocoons are placed into a container.

Blocks of Wood with drilled holes

It is not possible to harvest cocoons from drilled holes in solid blocks of wood. Even if tunnels can be opened at the back of the nest, cocoons are too fragile to be pushed out through the nesting tunnel. Neither is it possible to clean debris out of nesting tunnel, while bees are using nests, without destroying bees inside the nesting tunnel. At no time in the winter, spring or summer is

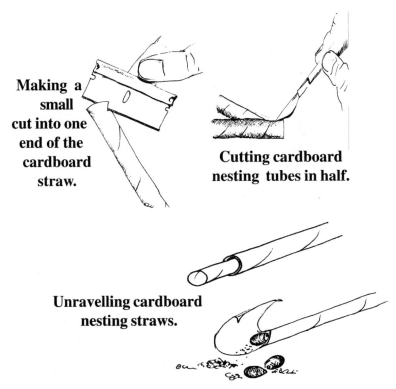

Making a small cut into one end of the cardboard straw.

Cutting cardboard nesting tubes in half.

Unravelling cardboard nesting straws.

the nesting tunnel free of bees since the nesting and emergence of bees overlaps. For example, some bees start nesting early in the spring while others are emerging from their nests. Thus, cleaning the nest with a drill in the spring is counter productive because drilling will destroy overwintering bees and newly laid eggs and developing young.

Alternating use of wood blocks with drilled holes

In spring, prior to bee emergence from the nest, place nesting block in cardboard box and tape box shut. Ensure that all holes in the box are darkened and taped shut to eliminate light entering the box. In other words make the box lightproof. Then create one exit hole for bees by pushing a pencil through a sidewall, at the base of box. Bees will emerge from the nest, go to the only source of light coming into the box and exit from this box. If box is placed outside in the sunshine, some mason bees may learn to recognize this small entrance hole to their natal nest and enter and use the nests inside the box. Place box in a carport or shed with open doors, where it is relatively dark. This will make it less likely for bees to go back to used nest inside the box. Bees generally do not go back into a box that is placed into a dark location if other nests are readily available for emerging females. If nests are scarce outside the box, bees will tend to find the punctured hole in the box and find the old nest.

6.2 CLEANING NESTS

Why

The main reason for cleaning nests and cocoons is hygiene. Bees prefer clean nests, and clean nests result in plentiful and healthy bees. After just one year, every nest contains old cocoon debris, mud particles, dead bees and parasites, including pollen feeding mites. Cleaning nests is an important part of managing your mason bees.

When

The best time to clean mason bee nests is from October to December. At this time adults are fully developed and sturdy enough inside their cocoons and will withstand the removal and cleaning process. Bees, be-

Mason bee cocoons covered in mites.

tween the months of September and December, do not emerge from their cocoons if held at room temperature. During these months, bees go through physiological changes required for their development. However, after December, bees can emerge in less than 24 hours at room temperature. If nests are cleaned and cocoons are harvested after December, limiting the number of hours that cocoons are kept at room temperature is necessary. Once bees emerge, they cannot be kept alive until spring. The time taken to process cocoons can be length-

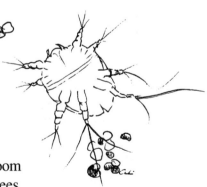

Pollen feeding mites.

ened if completed under cooler temperatures. By February, in particular male mason bees require only about 2-3 hours at 20°C (68°F) to emerge from their cocoons. Thus, it is safer to clean the nests and prepare the bees for storage in October.

How

After the cocoons have been removed from trays, soak the nesting trays in water to soften mud. Use a scrubbing brush with lots of water to remove mud and debris adhering to the nest. A brief 1-2 minute soak in 0.05% bleach [add 15 ml (1 tbs) of bleach (5% sodium hypochlorite) to 4 L (4 quarts or 16 cups of warm water] solution kills adhering bacteria and fungi. Rinse well with running water to remove all traces of bleach. Check that all bleach has been removed by smelling the wood.

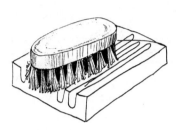

Scrubbing brush for cleaning trays.

6.3 CLEANING COCOONS

Cleaning cocoons can prevent disease from spreading from one bee to the next and can keep the young of the following year from becoming contaminated. Cocoons can be cleaned in water since these are buoyant and repel water. Excessive soaking may decrease their water- proofing.

Why

An advantage of harvesting and cleaning is that cocoons can be inspected and their contents determined. Diseased and parasitised cocoons can be examined, identified, and removed. Removal of suspect cocoons prevents escalating problems with disease and parasites. After cleaning, good quality cocoons can be separated from parasitised cocoons and prepared for the following spring. It is recommended to clean all cocoons, including those cocoons that are not covered in mites, since it increases the chance of identifying wasp parasitized and other diseased cocoons.

When

The best time to clean cocoons is when they are harvested in the fall. At harvest time, the cocoons are placed into large containers such as a 4 L (4 quarts or 8 cups) ice cream bucket. Avoid crushing the cocoons by minimizing the cocoon layers. Do not heap them deeper than 5 - 8 cm (2 - 3"). They are normally covered in faecal pellets and dried mud from nest partitions. Both the mud and faecal pellets can easily be washed off. If you live in coastal regions, expect cocoons to be covered with mites.

How

Washing cocoons is a relatively easy procedure, although somewhat time consuming. Note: Never use soap or detergent since soaplike materials will go through a cocoon and kill the bee inside just like the action of insecticidal soaps.

First, mud is removed by placing the cocoons into a 4 L (4 quarts or 8 cups) bowl of tepid water. Wet the cocoons by gently rolling and moving them through the water in a bowl. At first, mud falls away from cocoons and sinks to the bottom of container. Let cocoons sit for 5 to 15 minutes in the water, occasionally stirring them to ensure cocoons are well wetted down. Scoop them out of the bowl and place them in a large sieve. Place a strainer into the sink to prevent losing cocoons down the drain. Throw out the dirty water and throw the debris of mud and sand into the garbage. Some of the debris will be parasitic mites.

Second, mites are removed from the cocoons. Prepare a bleach solution (approximately 0.05%) by adding 15 ml (1 tbs) of bleach (5% sodium hypochlorite) to 4 L (4 quarts or 16 cups) of warm water. Lower the sieve containing the cocoons into the bowl.

Cocoons are first placed into a bowl of tepid water.

Submerging the cocoons into bleach will further wet them down and remove remaining particles and mites adhering to them. Lightly agitate the cocoons with your hand to make sure cocoons and mud are well wetted for easier removal of both mud and debris.

Set up a washing system so that water runs in at one side of a bowel, past cocoons contained inside the sieve, and out of bowl at opposite side of the bowl. Set water level in bowl below edge of sieve. This will prevent cocoons from going into the sink. Look closely at the surface of the water for a decreasing number of reddish

A sieve is used to rinse cocoons free of debris and mites.

mites that float away during the washing process. If there is inadequate water supply skip this stage.

After 10 minutes of this washing process, gently circulate cocoons in tepid water and leave them under running (tepid) water for another 5 min. Drain them in the sieve and turn them onto several layers of WHITE paper towels. Place an extra layer of white paper towels over the cocoons and wet it down. After an hour, remove towelling from cocoons. Look for tiny orange spots on the paper. If there are less than 10 mites per 6.5 cm^2 (10 per square inch), the first washing was a success. Additional washings are needed to lower the mite count to less than 5 mites / 6.5 cm^2 (5 per square inch), which is optimal. Two washings are usually required to remove most mites.

When the majority of mites have been removed, cocoons can be placed on another set of clean paper towels for drying. After an hour, most water will have evaporated. Cocoons can now be sorted to determine whether they are filled with parasitic wasps or mason bees.

Separating out parasitised cocoons

Since any parasite can devastate populations of bees it is recommended to keep parasites to a minimum. The easiest way to control parasitism is to remove cocoons containing the parasitic wasps.

Cocoons with adult mason bees are firm to touch and dark-grey in colour. Cocoons that are parasitised by wasps

White paper towel used to assess mite levels on cocoons after cocoons have been washed.

are usually lighter in colour, empty in appearance, and less firm and 'crispy' to touch. Sort, and place abnormal cocoons in a separate container with a clear lid. Store container with questionable cocoons in a cool place such as an unheated garage. In the spring, bring container inside and keep at room temperature. Insects will eventually develop and emerge. If cocoons contain tiny parasitic wasps (about 1/10th the size of a mosquito) cool down in fridge for 30 min. and destroy temporarily immobilized wasps. If the cocoons contain mason bees, cool down in fridge for 30 min. and release outside.

Each infested cocoon contains about 60 developing wasps, usually in the pre-pupae stage (undeveloped wasp). If a parasitised cocoon escapes detection, adult wasps emerge in May and June. These wasps enter the bees' nest to parasitize developing bees. Every three weeks, adult wasps emerge and parasitize additional developing bees. This process continues until the end of the warm weather or until bee nests are taken down and placed into storage.

6.4 WINTER COCOON STORAGE

Store cleaned and air-dried cocoons in a cardboard box, cushioned with toilet tissue. Place the box in a metal box or coffee container to prevent mice from eating the cocoons. Puncture one or two small holes into metal container for air circulation and to prevent cocoons from becoming mouldy. Mold grows on cocoons if they are stored wet and there is insufficient air circulation inside storage box.

In spring, mold can be removed from cocoons if bees have not started emerging from their cocoons. Wash the cocoons in a

Container with cocoons suspected to be infested with parasitic wasps.

bath of about 0.05% bleach [add 15 ml (1 tbs) of bleach (5% sodium hypochlorite) to 4 L (4 quarts or 16 cups of warm water]. Rinse several times with water to remove bleach from cocoons, and air-dry.

Cocoons can be placed in a refrigerator to prevent mason bees from emerging before bloom. The transfer of cocoons from outside winter storage locations into a refrigerator is usually done early in February before warmer spring temperatures arrive. Normally on the NW coast of North America., temperatures begin to increase in February. Set temperatures of refrigerator at 2 - 4°C (36 - 39°F). This narrow temperature range is critical for prolonging the overwintering of bee cocoons. At a temperature above 4°C (39°F), even at 7°C (45°F) which would seem 'low', males will

Boxes suitable for storing mason bee cocoons.

emerge while inside the refrigerator. At temperatures below 2°C (36°F) bees are more likely to freeze, although mason bees naturally withstand below zero temperatures for a period of time during the winter months. Do not use a frost free refrigerator because humidity is too low for bees to survive. The older fridges that require defrosting every once in a while have humidity of 60% and are ideal for keeping live insects. If a frost-free fridge is the only type that is available, cocoons can be stored in a high humidity environment in a an airtight container, above a damp paper towel.

6.5 SETTING OUT COCOONS IN SPRING

Cocoons can either be set out early in the spring under natural conditions, emerged earlier than under natural conditions, or kept under cold storage conditions for emergence later than under natural conditions. If fruit trees bloom when bees emerge, simply set out cocoons and let nature take its course. If fruit trees bloom before bees emerge, bees can be warmed and emerged earlier than under natural conditions. If bloom, such as blueberry bloom, appears later than the natural emergence of mason bees, cocoons can be cooled to delay emergence of the bees.

Natural Emergence of cocoons

The natural emergence of bees from cocoons is a simple procedure, but some precautions are necessary. Cocoons require protection from birds and other predators that take advantage of unprotected cocoons and bees that are in the process of emerging from their cocoons. Cocoons also need protection from rain and direct sunlight. Sunlight may dry out or cook the bee inside the cocoon.

If the quantity of cocoons is less than 50, place cocoons into a small box. Place lid on box to protect cocoons. Cut a small hole into the box so that bees can exit the box. Place this box adjacent to the nesting structure under the roof of a nest. If the box is small, it could be tucked into the nesting unit. Do not use boxes that have been used for pesticides, or petroleum products, as the residue in these boxes may kill the newly emerged mason bees. Even washing boxes free of residue may not completely remove these deadly insecticides.

If harvested cocoons consist of thousands of cocoons, place them in several boxes to prevent crushing. Wooden boxes can also be used as emerging boxes. The wood absorbs the sun's heat, warms up the cocoons and speeds the bees' emergence. At the same time, a wooden box protects bees from rain and predators. Separate cocoons with layers of toilet tissue to prevent cocoons from laying on top of one another. If any mites remain on the cocoon, separation from other cocoons is an advantage since these mites are likely to infest only the one bee…the resident of the infested cocoon.

Emerging bees earlier than under natural conditions

Mason bees can be emerged earlier than under natural conditions by placing cocoons into a warm and moist environment to speed up emergence.

Weather is a large factor in whether your bees will successfully mate and produce offspring. Poor weather conditions could be critical if cocoons are emerged during the early spring period. If bees emerge during a long period of inclement weather, they usually die since bees cannot forage for food. Healthy mason bees are able to stand several rainy days without feeding. Cold temperatures prevent foraging and gathering of nectar and pollen. Thus, it is advisable to divide bee cocoons into four groups to decrease the risk of losing all bees to inclement weather. Emerge one group of bees every 4 - 7 days. Emerged bees can be kept in the fridge for a few days and released when sunny.

Set up an artificial emergence box by placing toilet tissue in a plastic (transparent or translucent) container. Cut out part of the lid and glue screen material over hole. Loosely place cocoons on top of paper inside plastic container. Close container with modified screened lid. Place container with cocoons in a warm room held at a temperature of 20 - 25°C (68 - 77°F). An alternative is to create a smaller incubator by using a picnic cooler. Place a warm water bottle into a cooler and place container with the cocoons on top of warm water bottle. Place a damp towel over screened lid to maintain a high water moisture content in the surrounding air. Most bees emerge in the first 2-3 days. Do not use the oven or microwave to warm bees.

Under controlled conditions, at 24°C (75°F) and 50 - 60% humidity, cocoons require less than 1 week to emerge. Males emerge during the first couple of days, followed by females.

When to set out mason bees emerged early in the spring
Most bees usually emerge within 3 - 4 days, the majority emerge within 48 hours. After 24 - 48 h, or when significant number of bees have emerged, set container out near your nesting units. It is important to first cool bees to about 15°C to prevent them from flying off, never to be seen again. Set container with cocoons and bees into a fridge for about 15 - 30 min. Then, set this cooled container inside an open cardboard box, on its side, in the vicinity of nesting units early in the morning before temperatures increase to 15°C. By evening, most emerged bees will have left the container. Replace lid onto container and re-incubate to emerge remaining bees. After one week, check for cocoons that still have their contents. Collect these cocoons and emerge as noted in Chapter 6.3 which deals with parasitised cocoons.

Setting mason bees out later in spring
When late spring bloom, such as high bush blueberry, first appears, place cocoons into a box as described under Section 6.5 -Natural emergence of cocoons.

Chapter 7
Mason Bees
and Their Relatives

Mason bees belong to one of seven families of bees within the Order Hymenoptera. Six of these families consist of solitary bees and one of social bees. The six families of solitary bees comprise 119 genera and 3996 species. This chapter will include an introduction to one family of solitary bees (Megachilidae), and the one family of social bees (Apidae).

Both mason bees and leafcutter bees are grouped in the Family Megachilidae. Further, leafcutter bees are grouped into the Genus *Megachile* and mason bees are grouped into the Genus *Osmia*. Honey bees and bumble bees are grouped within the Family Apidae.

7.1 SOLITARY BEES

Solitary bees live just as their name implies -alone, and not in a colony. These bees live in the ground, above ground, within vegetation or on bare ground.

59

Solitary bees can be divided into renters, excavators, or builders. Renters use wood cavities, soil cavities, cracks in rocks, snail shells and plant galls, and small holes burrowed by beetles or other animals. Excavators excavate into the ground, vertical banks, stems or wood. Builders build on rock surfaces, stones or stems.

Often ground nesting bees nest in an area with suitable nesting soil characterized by its slope, texture and compactness. Thousands of bees may nest in these areas, each with its own nest compartment. Although these bees live in close proximity, they are not social. They do not cooperate in rearing their young and thus do not share nests. Some bee species may use the same or communal tunnels, but they tend to their own nests.

The General Life Cycle of Solitary Bees

Adult solitary bees emerge from early spring to late summer, depending on species, elevation, climate and location.

During spring through the summer, adults emerge from their nest and mate. A mated female then searches for a nest site and food (nectar and pollen). She provisions her nest with pollen and nectar stores on which she lays an egg. She then plugs up her nest cell and repeats this process daily until she dies.

Foragers may live anywhere from a few weeks to a few months. The shorter life span is more common. Many predators, such as birds and spiders, kill and eat bees, which makes foraging a dangerous task. Each egg develops into a larva which feeds on the pollen and nectar stores. Larva then develops into a pupa, and then into an adult. Development from egg to pre-pupa occurs during the summer months. Depending on species, the pre-pupa continues its development to the adult bee (as in *Osmia lignaria*, or development stops and overwinters in the pre-pupa stage (as in the leafcutter bee *Megachile rotundata*). The pre-pupae continues it development to adult during the following spring.

Family Megachilidae

It is a very large family, present throughout the world. The females carry pollen packed into a brush of hairs called a scopa underneath their abdomen. These bees also carry material into the nest to build cell partitions

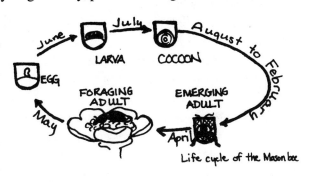

Life cycle of the Mason bee

and cell linings from outside. Material may be pieces of leaves, petals, chewed leaf pulp, resin, mud, pebbles, or hairs shaved from plants.

Genera *Osmia*

The *Osmia* genus or mason bees is one genera within the Family Megachlidae. The majority of mason bees are renters, they nest in existing cavities. Most use masticated leaf pulp and some use mud to plug up their nest. This genus is a group of black or metallic green, blue or blue-green bees. The nesting habits of *Osmia* are diverse. Some excavate burrows in the soil, while others use previously excavated burrows of other insects, and even empty snail shells. Bees also use natural nesting holes such as the hollow stems of water reeds (*Juncus spp*). Other bee species create nests in hollow stems by removing the pith from plants such as elderberry, and stems of the carrot family.

61

A common, large and abundant *Osmia* species in North America is *Osmia lignaria*. *Osmia lignaria* can be found from British Columbia to Quebec and the New England states, and as far south as California, Oklahoma and Georgia. The eastern sub-species is known as *Osmia lignaria lignaria* Say, and the western sub-species is known as *Osmia lignaria propinqua* Cresson. *Osmia ribifloris*

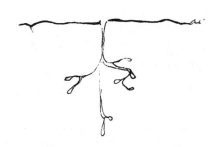

Ground nesting bees use excavated holes as their nests.

biedermannii Michener is another common early spring pollinator. One characteristic is that it has much longer hairs than *Osmia lignaria*. It naturally occurs in the very southern edge of Oregon, California and Utah south and east to California, Texas and northern Mexico.

Two non-native species of *Osmia* have recently been intentionally introduced into the United States of America: *Osmia cornuta* Latreile was imported from Europe, but has not been observed in any locality. However, *Osmia cornifrons* Radoszkowski, imported from Japan, has successfully established and has become feral in parts of the United States. *Osmia cornuta* can be recognized by its dense black hairs on the head and abdomen and red hairs on the abdomen.

Osmia texana

A smaller species of *Osmia*, *Osmia texana* Cresson that emerges during the summer months is under study in Victoria, Vancouver Island (British Columbia) by Rex Welland. He wrote the following description for inclusion in this book:

"*O. texana* is a native solitary bee. It emerges at time of blackberry bloom when the majority *of O. lignaria* have died. In Victoria, British Columbia, *O. texana* emerges in the beginning of May and remains active until early August. *O. texana* forages at warmer temperature than *O. lignaria*, and does not become active until daytime temperature reach 21°C (70°F).

In the Pacific North West, it is approximately half the size of *O. lignaria*. But size seems to vary from one region to another. In California it is usually smaller while in the Rocky Mountain regions it is usually larger. Females are a metallic black/blue in colour. The male has similar colouration except that the hairs on its body are golden-red - especially in the sun. Like *O. lignaria, O. texana* readily accepts man-made nest boxes. The only difference is the size of the hole. *O. texana* prefers a 4 mm (5/32") diameter hole. The female provisions the chambers with a pollen-nectar mix, on each of which she deposits an egg. Like *O. lignaria, O. texana*, partitions off each chamber. Unlike *O. lignaria, O. texana* often includes slivers of wood in the final plug. Again, the stages of their lifecycle are similar. But with one exception. *O. texana* are 'parsivoltine'. That is, some emerge the following season while some remain in their cocoons for a second year before they emerge. Thus, if the end-plug remains closed during the spring and summer, it may mean that these bees will emerge the following year, not that they are dead.

O. texana can be found in British Columbia and Alberta, to Ohio and New York, and south to California.

It is known to visit trailing blackberry, red elderberry, boysenberry and blueberry flowers."

Genus *Megachile*

These bees are non-metallic, black bees that cut leaves and sometimes petals (e.g. rose) to line and cap each cell. There are about 115 species of leafcutter bee in North America. About 22 species occur in Western Canada.

Megachile rotundata Fabricius is an alfalfa leafcutter bee that originates from Eurasia. This species is used in the commercial seed production of alfalfa. The female *M. rotundata* has silvery gray hairs on the underside of its abdomen. Other female leafcutter bees usually have a golden, tan, or black scopa.

M. rotundata overwinters in the pre-pupae stage. During late spring and early summer, temperatures are sufficiently warm for pre-pupae to develop into adults. Under controlled incubation conditions, development time to the adult stage is 20 to 31 days at 30°C (86°F). Adults emerge and start pollinating at temperatures of 18°C (64°F).

Commercially available nesting materials for the leafcutter bees were first made out of grooved wooden pine boards that were stacked to make a series of nests. Polystyrene is a more recent innovation. Polystyrene grooved boards and nesting holes moulded into solid polystyrene blocks are both used today. However, polystyrene is one of the least preferred nest materials used by *O. lignaria,* the mason bee.

Naming Megachilid Bees

Since there are many species of solitary bees, few can easily be identified and few have common names. Nevertheless, using a simple description of the adult together with a description of the nest plug, the genus of the bee can often be determined. The nest plug is made from either mud, masticated leaves, resins or a mixture of these materials (Table 1). The bee is described as either striped or metallic blue/green. The diameter of the nesting tunnel is an additional feature used to identify a bee to genus.

Table 1. Description of some solitary bee nest-plug construction and adult bees that provide preliminary identification to genera of solitary bees (after Hallett, 2001 and modified by W. Stephens; J. Cane).

NEST PARTITION CONSTRUCTION	ADULT	FAMILY	GENERA
Polyester	Variable	COLLETIDAE	Hylaeus
Leaf cuttings	Striped	MEGACHILIDAE	Megachile
Mastic of leaves mixed with resins & pebbles	Striped	MEGACHILIDAE	Megachile
Resins, sand & pebbles	Striped	MEGACHILIDAE	Chelosto-moides
Soil & or mastic of leaves and sometimes resins.	Metallic *(not all)*	MEGACHILIDAE	Osmia
Resins and stones	Not metallic	MEGACHILIDAE	Anthidium
Pithy partitions and cap	Variable	APIDAE (Xylocopinae)	Ceratina Hoplotis

7.2 SOCIAL BEES

Social insects are insects that work together to reproduce. They are present in large numbers in a nest and gather food, defend the nest and care for the young. Examples of social insect are some bees and wasps, and all ants and termites. Honey bees and bumble bees are social bees.

Honey bees

Honey bees live together in a colony that may reach a size of 60,000 bees in the summer. There is one queen that lays the eggs of a colony. The remaining bees of a colony are workers and drones. Workers are underdeveloped females that were not fed the large amounts of royal jelly usually given to developing queens. Drones are males.

Honey bee workers do all types of tasks. Inside the hive, young bees begin by tending and feeding the young brood and cleaning out cells. As workers age, foraging becomes their major task. Depending on the needs of a colony the workers become foragers for pollen, nectar, water, or plant resins (propolis). They

Honey bees and their hive.

continue their foraging tasks until they die. In the summer it can be as short as 14 days since foraging is a dangerous task. Birds, insects, spiders, skunks, bears and man all prey on bees and their nest contents. Unlike workers, the males of a colony, or drones spend most of their life inside the colony. Drones mature while inside the colony. On maturity, they fly out of the nest to find virgin queens. New queens mate on the wing with several drones. Drones die upon mating.

Bumble bees

Bumble bees also are social bees. A colony of bumble bees works together as a cohesive unit to find food, store food, produce workers, queens and drones. Like honey bees there is usually one queen but only a few hundred workers.

Bumble bees are important as early spring pollinators and as alpine pollinators in North America. They visit many flowers per minute. Because of their size and 'fuzziness', they do an excellent job of transferring pollen from one flower to another. Different bumble bee species appear at different times of the spring, but because colony life extends over several months, several species are present at the same time of the year.

Where do bumble bees live?

In nature, bumble bees may nest underground, in a cavity alongside roots, or in a tree cavity created by other animals. In suburbia, bees nest in walls with fibreglass insulation or in abandoned bedding. Bird boxes with abandoned bird nests are also used by bumble bees as are abandoned mouse nests.

The bumble bee life cycle

When blossoms first appear early in spring, a large mated bumble bee queen emerges from her hibernation cavity. She will first search for nectar to replenish her energy. Then, she searches for a summer nest. When she has found a nest site, a new queen collects nectar and pollen from flowers. At the nest, she mixes pollen with nectar and forms a lump of food for her young. When the pollen lump is 'large enough', she lays a cluster of eggs on this pollen lump and buries them within the surface of the pollen lump. The pollen lump may be as large as the first digit of a finger or thumb. She then begins a 20-30 day brooding period, like a broody hen. Bumble bees generate heat by vibrating their thoracic muscles. Heat produced keeps the eggs warm which then develop into larva. The larvae feed on the pollen-nectar lump. Each larva then transform into pupa and emerges as an adult bumble bee. This transformation from egg to adult takes about 16-25 days.

The size of bumble bee workers depends on the amount of food available during their larval stage of development. Often, the early workers of some species are 1/3 the size of a worker honey bee, whereas bumble bee workers in late spring may approach the size of three honey bee workers. In some species last workers of the season also are very small. The queen is usually the length to the first segment of your thumb. Workers may approach the size of queens in times when food is plentiful.

When young bumble bees emerge, their duties are in-house until they mature to become foragers. After a few days to a week, foragers emerge from the nest and begin foraging for food. When the worker bumble bees begin foraging, the queen stays in the nest and lays more eggs which she and her workers incubate.

By early summer, the number of workers may reach 150 individuals. The largest known bumble bee colony (east coast of north America) of the temperate zone had approximately 3,000 individuals (east coast of North America). In the middle of the summer, when the colony is large, the colony produces new queens and drones. About one month later, virgin queens emerge from the nest, feed on nectar and mate with the drones. Once drones emerge they do not re-enter the nest. They stay over night on flowers and amongst flowers and foliage. Drones can be recognized by their abundant yellow hairs on their faces, longer antennae and lack of pollen baskets.

In the meantime, the newly mated queens find a hibernation cavity and remain there until the following spring. The hibernation hole may be a very small cavity in soil or in other locations such as peat moss. The original colony eventually dwindles, and the remaining bumble bees die.

Bumble bees emerging from their hibernating hole.

Bumble bees nesting in a hollow amongst tree roots.

...." I devoted a month's salary to the acquisition of the book. I had to resort to miracles of econonmy for some time to come before making up the enormous deficit.

The book was devoured; there is no other word for it. In it, I learned the name of my black Bee; I read for the first time various details of the habits of insects: I found, surrounded in my eyes with a sort of halo, the revered names of Reaumur, Huber and Leon Dufour; and, while I turned over the pages for the hundredth time, a voice within me seemed to whisper: 'You also shall be of their company!' "

In 'The Mason-Bees' by J. H. Fabre, 1916, pp 9-10.
[Fabre refers to 'Histoire naturelle des animaux articules, by de Castelnau, E.Blanchard and Lucas]

Glossary

Alfalfa leafcutter bee. An introduced Eurasion species *Megachile rotundata*, belonging to the leafcutter family Megachilidae, that forms the basis for a multimillion-dollar agribusiness for pollinating alfalfa. The bee is easily managed in straws, boards, and styrofoam nesting blocks.

Anther. The pollen containing part of the floral stamens where the pollen grains are produced.

Biodiversity. The variability of living creatures within a habitat.

Bumble bee. The common name for any bee in the *Genus Bombus*. These are large hairy, often black, white and yellow, or reddish social bees.

Cross-pollination. The transfer of pollen from the anthers of one plant to a recipient stigma of another plant and may result in fertilization and fruit set.

Hive. An artificial nest for honey bees provided by beekeepers.

Hymenoptera. The order of insects which includes the sawflies, wasps , ants and bees.

Mason bee. The common name given to any bee in the *Genus Osmia* and belonging to the Megachilidae bee family.

Nectar. A liquid mixture of sugars secreted by the nectaries of plants.

Pollen. Microscopic particles in anthers that contain the male sperm nuclei.

Pollination. The process of moving pollen from the anthers of one flower to the stigma of another.

Queen. The principle or only egg-laying female in a social colony, who does little or no foraging.

Social bees. Bees that live together in a communal nest and share foraging and nest duties.

Solitary. A female bee or wasp that lives alone in a nest of her own construction which she provisions.

Stigma. The female receptive portion of the style.

Stamen. The male structure bearing the pollen grains in a flower.

Style. The middle connective portion of a female flower.

Guide to Further Reading

Bees

Michener, C. D. 1974. **The Social Behavior of the Bees** – A Comparative Study. Harvard University Press, Cambridge, Mass. *A technical book that compares the behaviour of social and solitary bees. [b&w]*

O'Toole, C. and A. Raw. 1991. **Bees of the World.** Blandford Publishing, London. UK. *Excellent overview of bees, both solitary and social. [colour]*

Muller, A., A. Krebs and F. Amiet. 1997. **Bienen.** Weltbild Verlag GmbH, Augsburg. ISBN 3-89440-241-5 [in German]. *Clear & vivid photographs of nesting solitary bees, their nest structures and habitat. [colour]*

Solitary Bees

Bosch, J. and W. P. Kemp. **How to Manage the Blue Orchard Bee, *Osmia lignaria*, as an Orchard Pollinator.** Sustainable Agriculture Network (SAN), Washington, DC. (in press).

Fabre, J.H. 1916. **The Mason-Bees.** Dodd, Mead & Co. NY.

Griffen, B. 1993. **The Orchard Mason Bee.** Knox Cellars Publishing, Bellingham.WA. *An introduction to keeping orchard mason bees. [b&w]*

Leaf cutter Bees

Richards, K. W. 1984. **Alfalfa Leafcutter Bee Management in Western Canada.** Agriculture Canada Pub. No. 1495 / E. Comm Branch, Ag. Can. Ottawa. *Overview of commercial management of alfalfa leafcutter bees. [b&w]*

Bumble bees

Alford, D. V. 1978. **The life of the Bumble bee.** Davis-Poynter, London. *A naturalists' overview of bumble bees. [b&w]*

Heinrich, B. 1979. **Bumble Bee Economics.** Harvard Univ. Press, Cambridge, Mass. *Overview bumble bees and their lives. [b&w]*

Von Hagen, E. 1994. **Hummeln.** Weltbild Verlag GmbH, Augsburg. [in German] *Excellent colour photographs of habitat, nests and bumble bee species. [colour]*

Honey bees

Seeley, T. D. 1995. **The Wisdom of the Hive:** The Social Physiology of Honey Bees. Harvard University Press, Cambridge, Mass. *In-depth look at the behaviour of honey bees. [b&w]*

Winston, M. L. 1987. **The Biology of the Honey Bee.** Harv.Univ.Press, Camb, Mass. *An overview of honey bee biology. [b&w]*

Winston, M. L. 1992. **Killer Bees.** The Africanized honey bees in the Americas. Harvard University Press Cambridge Mass. *All about the Africanized honey bee. [b&w]*

Pollination

Free, J. B. 1993. **Insect Pollination of Crops.** Academic Press, London. *Technical details on the pollinator requirements of crops. [b&w]*

Buchmann, S. L. and G. P. Nabhan. 1996. **The Forgotten Pollinators.** Island Press / Shearwater Books, Washington DC. *Stories from around the globe emphasizing the importance of pollinators.*

Dogterom, M. H. 1999. **Pollination by Four Species of Bees on High Bush Blueberry.** PhD thesis. Simon Fraser University.

Gardening

Henderson, C. L. 1992. **Landscaping for Wildlife.** Minnesota's
    Bookstore St. Paul M.N. *Detailed information on how to make our
    land more attractive to wildlife. Extensive list of good food
    plants for bees, moths and birds and other animals. [colour]*

General

Norden, B.B. 1991. **The Bee.** Stewart, Tabori & Chang Inc. NY.*A pop-up
    book on social and solitary bees for adults and children. [colour]*

Forey, P. and C. Fitzsimons. 1987. **An Instant Guide to Insects.** Gramercy
    Books, NY. *How to identify insects. [colour]*

Identification of Solitary Bees - Technical

Banaszak, J. and L. Romasenko. 1998. **Megachilid Bees of Europe.**
    Wydawnictwo Uczelniane WsP w Bydgoszczy. [in English] ISBN
    83 -7096-268-8. *Detailed descriptions and technical sketches of
    Megachilid solitary bees. [b&w]*
Michener, C. D., R. J. McGinley and B. N. Danforth. 1994. **The Bee
    Genera of North and Central America.** Smithsonian Institution
    Press, Washington. *Technical book on how to identify bees to
    genera. [b&w]*
Mitchell, T. B. 1962. **Bees of the Eastern United States Volume II.** The
    North Carolina Agricultural Experiment Station. *Technical book
    on how to identify families Megachilidae, Anthophoridae,
    Xylocopidae and Apidae. [b&w]*
Stephen. W. P. 1957. **Bumble Bees of Western America (Hymenoptera:
    Apoidea).** Technical Bulletin 40. Agricultural Experimental
    Station, Oregon State College. Corvallis. *Technical book with
    range maps and line drawings of colour variations of some
    species.*

Index

77